A Kid's Book of Experiments with

SOUND

SURPRISING Science Experiments

Robert Gardner
and
Joshua Conklin

W9-BFU-098

3 4028 09035 9150
HARRIS COUNTY PUBLIC LIBRARY

J 534.078 Gar
Gardner, Robert
A kid's book of experiments
with sound

$11.70
ocn918562862

Enslow Publishing

101 W. 23rd Street
Suite 240
New York, NY 10011
USA

enslow.com

Published in 2016 by Enslow Publishing, LLC
101 W. 23rd Street, Suite 240, New York, NY 10011

Copyright © 2016 by Enslow Publishing, LLC

All rights reserved.

No part of this book may be reproduced by any means without the written permission of the publisher.

Library of Congress Cataloging-in-Publication Data

Gardner, Robert, 1929- author.
 A kid's book of experiments with sound / Robert Gardner and Joshua Conklin.
    pages cm. — (Surprising science experiments)
 Audience: Ages 9+
 Audience: Grades 4 to 6.
 Includes bibliographical references and index.
 ISBN 978-0-7660-7209-1 (library binding)
 ISBN 978-0-7660-7207-7 (pbk.)
 ISBN 970-0-7660-7208-4 (6-pack)
1. Sound—Experiments—Juvenile literature. 2. Science—Experiments—Juvenile literature. 3. Science projects—Juvenile literature. I. Conklin, Joshua, author. II. Title.
 QC225.5.G374 2016
 534.078—dc23
                                   2015029983

Printed in the United States of America

To Our Readers: We have done our best to make sure all website addresses in this book were active and appropriate when we went to press. However, the author and the publisher have no control over and assume no liability for the material available on those websites or on any websites they may link to. Any comments or suggestions can be sent by e-mail to customerservice@enslow.com.

Photo Credits: Throughout book: Wiktoria Pawlak/Shutterstock.com (lightbulbs), VLADGRIN/Shutterstock.com (science background), Aleksandrs Bondars/Shutterstock.com (colorful banners), vector-RGB/Shutterstock.com (arrows); cover, p. 1 © iStockphoto.com/Zhenikeyev (boy holding radio); Sapann-Design/Shutterstock.com (colorful alphabet); Login/Shutterstock.com (rainbow wheel); p. 4 MaszaS/Shutterstock.com; p. 10 lilyling1982/Shutterstock.com; p. 14 Jupiterimages/Photos.com/Thinkstock; p. 24 aerogondo2/Shutterstock.com; p. 25 Lisa Turay/Shutterstock.com; p. 29 Alenavlad/Shutterstock.com; p. 30 Vasiliy Koval/Shutterstock.com.

Illustration Credits: Accurate Art, Inc. c/o George Barile.

CONTENTS

Introduction

You began to hear sounds when you were only sixteen weeks old, still growing inside your mother. When you later entered the world, you started making noises of your own. Since then, you've learned to distinguish a cry from a laugh, a guitar from a drum, and a dog's bark from a cat's meow. But how much do you know about the sounds that surround you? In this book you will investigate how sound is made, how sound travels, and how sound can be altered. Let's get to work!

Making Sounds

From the call of a mourning dove at sunrise to the hoot of an owl at dusk, the day is filled with sound. But how is a sound created? Is the sound of a bat striking a ball made in the same way as the sound of a woodpecker striking a tree? Let's make sounds in different ways and explore this question.

Experiment 1: Making Sounds With Rulers and Tuning Forks

Things You Will Need:

- an adult
- ruler
- table or counter
- meterstick or yardstick
- rubber bands
- string
- drawer handle
- tuning forks
- rubber hammer or shoe heel
- glass of water
- sharp knife
- empty, open oatmeal box
- plastic wrap
- table salt
- cooking pot
- spoon
- friend who will sing

1. Find a 30 cm (1 ft) ruler. Hold one end of the ruler firmly against a table or counter. (See Figure 1.) Let most of the ruler hang over the table.

2. Pluck the free end of the ruler with your finger. Do you hear a sound?

3. In small steps, reduce the length of the ruler hanging over the table. After each step, pluck the free end of the ruler. As the length of the ruler hanging over the table shortens, what do you notice about the sound? Does its pitch change?

   The rate at which the ruler moves up and down after being plucked is called its frequency. Frequency is measured in vibrations per second. The unit used to measure frequency in science is called a hertz (Hz). A frequency of 1 vibration per second equals 1 Hz.

4. Repeat the experiment using a meterstick or yardstick. With most of the meterstick hanging over the table, you may not hear a sound when you pluck. Does the frequency increase as you shorten the meterstick's length?

5. Attach a rubber band to a drawer handle. Stretch the rubber band and pluck it. Does it make a sound? What can you observe about the rubber band while it is making a sound?

Figure 1

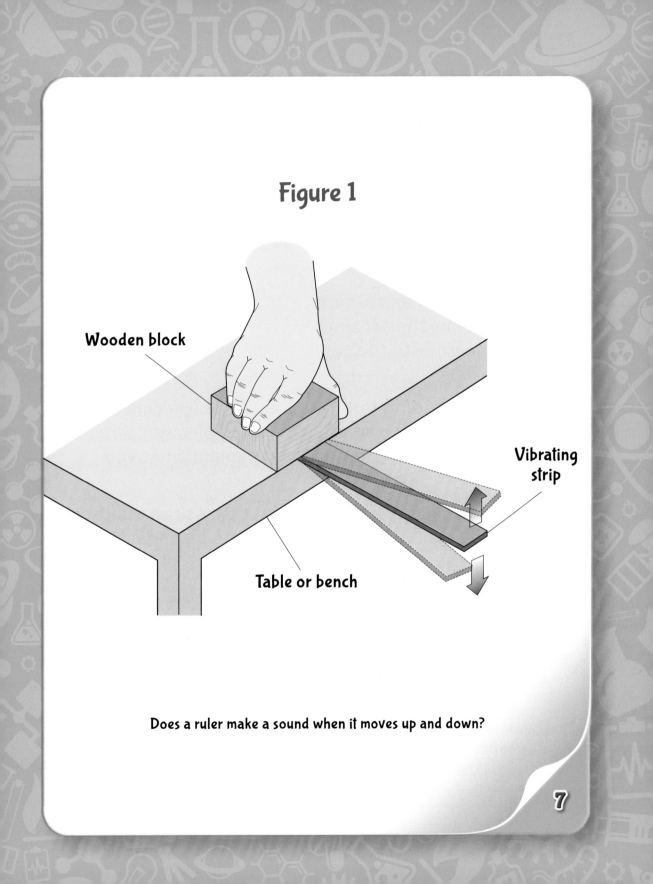

Wooden block

Vibrating strip

Table or bench

Does a ruler make a sound when it moves up and down?

6. Repeat this experiment with a long piece of string instead of a rubber band. Does it make a sound when you pluck it?

7. Hold the base of a tuning fork. Tap one of the tines with a rubber hammer. Or tap the tuning fork against the rubber heel of your shoe. Can you hear a sound?

8. Repeat the experiment with a tuning fork with longer or shorter tines. How does the sound compare with the sound made by the first tuning fork?

9. Strike a tuning fork with long tines. Quickly lower the ends of the tines into a glass of water. What do you notice? How can you explain what you saw?

10. Find an empty, open oatmeal box. **Ask an adult** to cut a small hole in the side of the box near the top (Figure 2).

11. Stretch a piece of plastic wrap over the open top of the box and use a rubber band to keep the plastic firmly stretched.

12. Sprinkle some table salt on the plastic wrap. Then hold a cooking pot upside down above (not touching) the plastic. Hit the bottom of the pot with a spoon. What happens to the salt crystals?

Figure 2

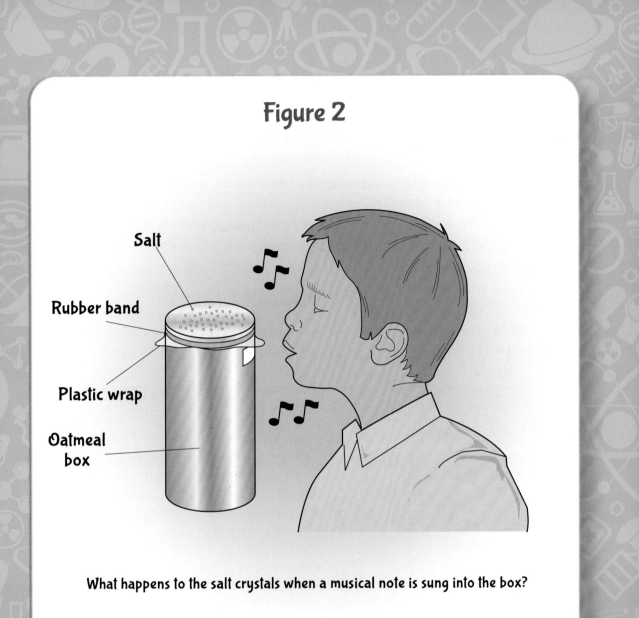

Salt

Rubber band

Plastic wrap

Oatmeal box

What happens to the salt crystals when a musical note is sung into the box?

13. Have a friend sing a number of different notes into the opening in the box. One or more notes should make the salt bounce up and down. What does that tell you about sound?

Making Sounds: An Explanation

You plucked a number of different items and each made a sound. While the specific sounds they made were different, did you notice that something was vibrating every time you heard a sound? The ruler, yardstick, rubber band, string, and tuning forks all vibrated (moved up and down or back and forth) and this vibration was the source of the sound. The faster something vibrates (the greater the frequency of vibration), the higher the pitch of the sound it makes.

Could the notes your friend sang also be caused by vibrations? In the next experiment we will explore further to find out.

You hear lots of sounds at a fireworks display and feel some of the vibrations!

Can You Feel Sound?

Have you ever had music playing loud enough that you could really feel the beat thumping in your bones? We saw in the previous experiment that sounds are caused by vibrations. But how loud does a sound have to be in order to be felt? Could the vibration be too slow or too fast to feel or even be heard? In this experiment we will further explore how to feel sound by making vibrations with music and voice.

Experiment 2:
How Does Sound Feel?

Things You Will Need:

- a radio
- large balloon
- twist tie
- a friend who can sing

1. Turn on a radio or music player with speakers and turn up the volume. (You might want to let a parent know why you are blasting music . . . it's for science!)

2. Blow up a large balloon. Seal its neck with a twist tie so air can't escape.

3. Hold the balloon gently with the fingertips of both hands (Figure 3a). Put the balloon against a speaker. Can you feel vibrations coming from the speaker?

4. Turn the music off. Hold the balloon close to your mouth. Sing or speak loudly. Can you feel the vibrations?

5. Sing a low note and then a high note. Can you feel a difference in the vibrations?

6. Ask a friend to sing a full octave (*do, re, me, fa, sol, la, ti, do*) into the balloon (Figure 3b). Can you feel a difference in the vibrations as the notes increase in pitch?

7. Hold the fingers of one hand on your voice box (larynx). Sing a note near the balloon. Can you feel the vibrations of your vocal cords? Can you feel them when you talk? Does singing or talking louder help?

Figure 3

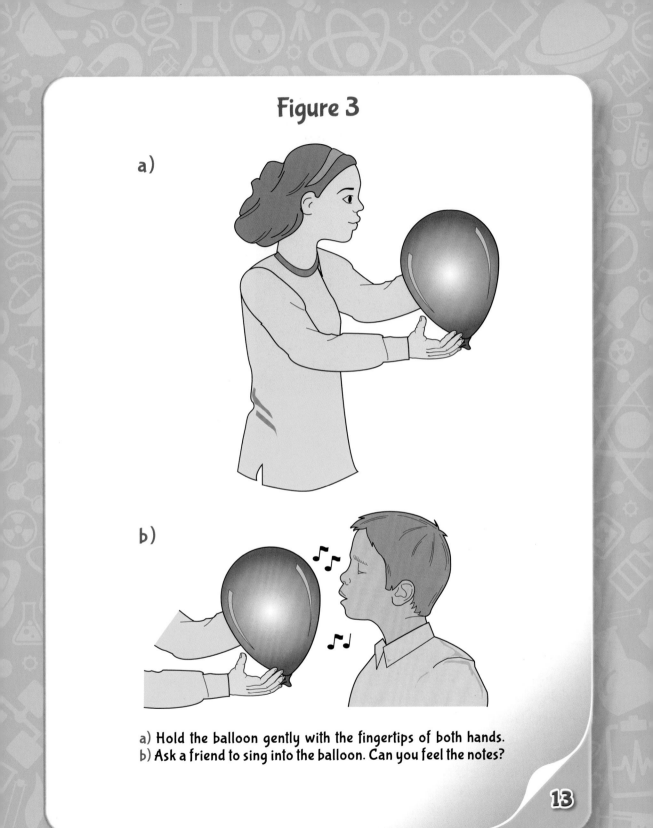

a) Hold the balloon gently with the fingertips of both hands.
b) Ask a friend to sing into the balloon. Can you feel the notes?

The vibrations in a singer's voice can even shatter glass

Can You Feel Sound? An Explanation

The sounds coming from the speakers or a voice made the air in the balloon vibrate. It is likely that you could feel the vibrations if the sounds were loud. You probably could feel the vibrations when your friend sang notes into the balloon. You may have felt the vibrations of your vocal cords when you sang or spoke.

Remember Experiment 1? You may not have heard anything when most of the yardstick was vibrating. If you did hear it, it had a very low pitch. Humans generally cannot hear sounds that are less than 20 Hz (or sounds that are vibrating at less than 20 times per second). The hearing range for humans is between 20 and 20,000 Hz. Few can hear sounds that vibrate at a frequency less than 20 Hz but some can hear frequencies above 20,000 Hz. Generally, as people grow older, their ability to hear high frequencies decreases.

Table 1 provides the hearing range of some animals. Many animals hear sounds we can't. A dolphin, for example, can't hear some of the low-pitched sounds we can but has a much greater ability to hear high-pitched sounds—nearly eight times as high!

Table 1:
The average hearing range of a number of animals.

Animal	Hearing range (Hz)
bat	1,000 to 120,000
cat	55 to 77,000
dog	64 to 44,000
dolphin	150 to 150,000
elephant	17 to 105,000
gerbil	56 to 60,000
horse	55 to 33,000

IDEAS for a Science Project

- Obtain a dog whistle with a frequency you can't hear. Does your dog respond to the whistle?

- Cup your hand behind one ear. Does it improve your hearing? If it does explain why it does.

How Sound Travels

When sitting across from a friend at a table, you can easily chat. If you were to step outside, you could yell back and forth from quite a distance, though the neighbors might get upset! In each instance the only thing between you and your friend is air. We know therefore that sound travels through air. What would happen if you were underwater or talking to each other through a wall? Let's do an experiment to learn more about how sound travels along other substances.

Experiment 3: What Kinds of Matter Will Conduct (Carry) Sound?

Things You Will Need:

- watch or small clock that ticks
- partner
- ruler
- pencil and paper
- drinking glass
- empty soda can
- long piece of lumber (such as a 2 x 4) and sawhorses, or a long wooden table
- dinner fork
- dinner knife
- soap and water

Let's compare how air conducts sound with other materials by using a watch or small clock that makes a tick every second.

1. Hold the metal (back) side of the watch against your ear. Slowly move the watch away from your ear and stop when you can no longer hear the ticks.

2. Hold the watch at that position. Have a partner measure and record the distance between the watch and your ear. It's probably a few centimeters.

3. Hold a drinking glass against your ear. Hold the metal (back) side of the watch against the other side of the glass. Can you hear the watch? Which do you think is a better conductor of sound, glass or air?

4. Hold one side of an empty soda can against your ear. Hold the watch against the other side. Is the metal a good conductor of sound?

5. Find a long piece of lumber, such as a 2 x 4, and rest it on sawhorses, or a long wooden table. Put your ear against one end of the board or table (Figure 4). Have a partner place the metal (back) side of the watch against the wood. It should be a few centimeters from your ear. Can you hear the ticks? Ask the partner to move the watch a few centimeters farther. Then listen for a tick.

Continue doing this until you can no longer hear the watch through the wood. Record the distance.

Over what distance could you hear the sound through wood? Is wood a better conductor of sound than air?

6. Tap the tines of a dinner fork with a dinner knife. Quickly hold the tines near your ear. Do you hear a ringing sound?

7. Clean the handle of the dinner fork with soap and water. Then hold the handle of the fork between your teeth. **Gently** tap the tines of the fork with a dinner knife. What do you hear? What can you conclude?

How Sound Travels: An Explanation

Most of the sounds we hear travel through air. But, as your experiments with the watch show, air is not a very good conductor of sound. You probably found that glass, metal, and wood are better sound conductors than air since you could hear the watch ticking from farther away.

The experiment with the dinner fork tested the conduction of sound through the bones of your skull. With the fork between your teeth, you probably found that the ringing was quite loud. It was louder than the ringing when the tines were near your ear. Bones and many other solids are better sound conductors than air.

Figure 4

VIEW FROM ABOVE

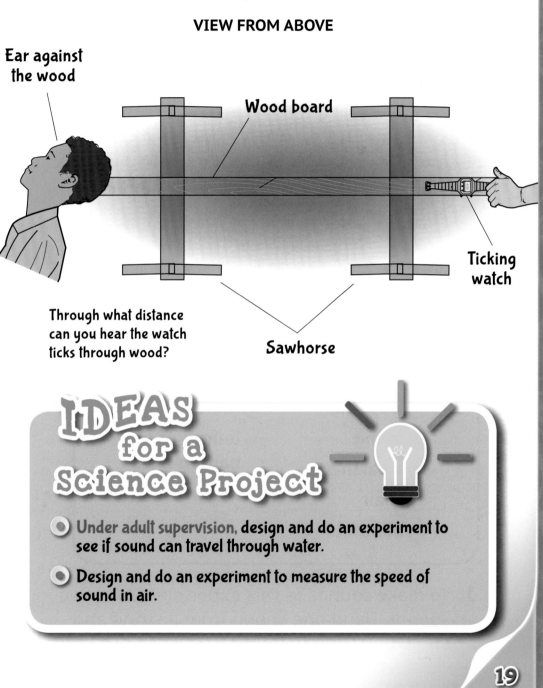

Ear against the wood

Wood board

Ticking watch

Sawhorse

Through what distance can you hear the watch ticks through wood?

IDEAS for a Science Project

- Under adult supervision, design and do an experiment to see if sound can travel through water.

- Design and do an experiment to measure the speed of sound in air.

Locating Sounds With One or Both Ears

Let's say a friend is calling you from inside your house. It probably won't take you long to locate her by following the sound of her voice. But what if your sister were playing the piano at the same time? What if you lost hearing in one ear? How do we locate the direction of sounds? Let's use an experiment to help find out.

Experiment 4: Locating the Source of Sounds

Things You Will Need:

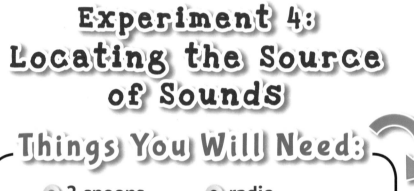

- 2 spoons
- string
- a partner
- chair
- blindfold
- radio
- length of old garden hose
- felt pen

1. To make sounds in this experiment, use two spoons. Hang one spoon from a string and strike it with the other spoon.

2. Have a partner sit in a chair in the center of a room. We'll call your partner the subject. Cover the subject's eyes with a blindfold. Tell the subject you are going to make a sound. Ask the subject to point to the sound as soon he or she hears it.

3. Stand about 2 m (6 ft) in front of the seated subject.

4. Make a sound using the spoons. Ask the subject to point to the sound.

5. Randomly move to different positions around the seated person. Make a sound at each position and ask the subject to point to the sound. How accurately can the subject locate the direction of the sound?

6. Repeat the experiment at a greater distance. Do you notice a difference in the subject's ability to locate sounds?

7. Repeat the experiment. But this time have the subject cover one ear with his hand. How well does the subject do using one ear?

8. Do the experiment once more. This time have a radio playing softly while you make sounds. How well does the subject do with a radio turned on?

9. Let's see how well the subject can detect whether a sound is from the right or left by using a piece of garden hose about 1.5 m (4 to 5 ft) long.

10. Measure and mark the center of the hose with a felt pen.

11. Have the subject hold the ends of the hose against his ears (Figure 5). The rest of the tube should be behind him. Scratch the tube with your fingernail. At what distance from the center can the subject tell whether the sound is from the left or the right?

Locating Sounds with One or Both Ears: An Explanation

Using both ears, a person can usually locate the direction of a sound quite accurately. Even doubling the distance to the sound usually makes little difference. With one ear, or with a radio turned on, the subject was probably much less successful. You were probably surprised to see the results when you scratched the hose. It's likely the subject could distinguish right from left when you scratched only a short distance from center.

The ability to locate a sound is made easier because the sound is slightly louder at the ear nearer the source, so the sound reaches the closer ear a bit sooner. Your body uses these clues to locate the sound. With only one ear or with a lot of background noise, these clues (loudness and time difference) are absent.

You may have noticed that some animals can turn their ears toward a sound. Some can also raise their ears. This is nature's way of helping them "capture" more sound or focus their hearing in a certain direction. Humans do something similar when they place a hand behind their ear to assist in hearing.

Figure 5

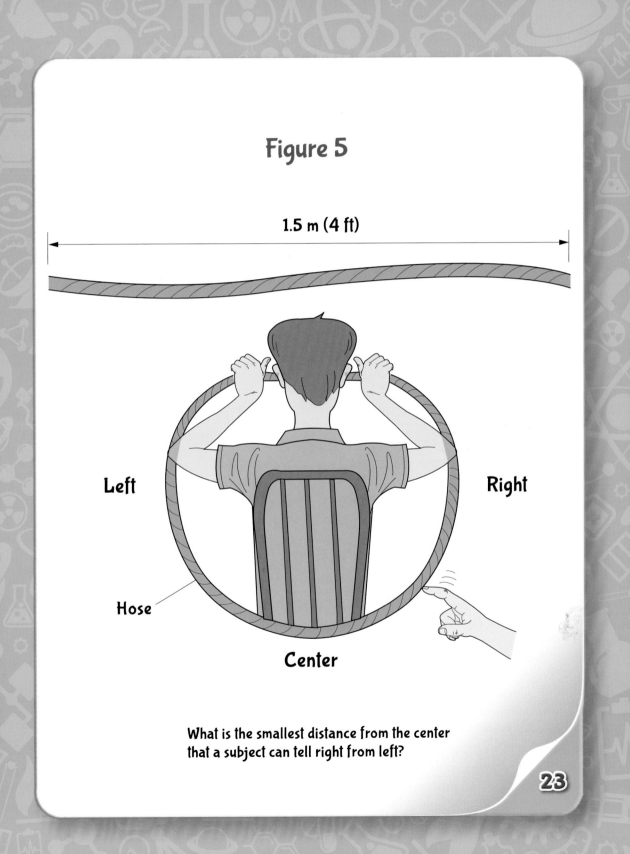

1.5 m (4 ft)

Left

Right

Hose

Center

What is the smallest distance from the center that a subject can tell right from left?

Hearing aids like the one seen here can improve a person's ability to hear words and music.

How Does Thickness Affect the Pitch of a Vibrating String?

We've learned about how sound is made, how sound travels, and how we hear and locate sounds. But what else helps shape the pitch of the sounds we hear? Does the thickness or heaviness of a string affect the rate at which it vibrates? You can find out by doing the next experiment.

Experiment 5:
Pitch and the Thickness
of a Vibrating String

Things You Will Need:

- an adult
- board approximately 5 cm (2 in) thick, 60 cm (2 ft) long, and 10 cm (4 in) wide
- hammer
- 2 nails
- ruler
- C-clamp
- old table or counter
- scissors
- thick and thin fishing line (often referred to as the "test" of the line; 6-lb test is thinner than 12-lb test)
- S-shaped metal hooks or two large, heavy-duty paper clips side by side
- plastic pail
- water
- quart jar or measuring cup
- large (thick) pencil or pen

1. Find a board approximately 5 cm (2 in) thick, 60 cm (2 ft) long, and 10 cm (4 in) wide. If you can't find such a board, **ask an adult** to cut one for you.

2. With the help of **an adult,** drive two nails partway into one end of the board (see Figure 6). The nails should be about 3 cm (1.5 in) apart.

3. Use a C-clamp to fasten the board to a table.

4. Cut a piece of both thick and thin fishing line about 90 cm (3 ft) long.

5. Tie one end of each line to the bottom of one of the nails (Figure 6).

6. Tie S-shaped metal hooks or two large, heavy-duty paper clips (side by side) to the other ends of the two lines (Figure 6).

7. Hang a plastic pail on the hook at the end of the thick fishing line. Pour a quart of water into the pail.

8. Place a large (thick) pencil or pen under the strings near the nails (Figure 6).

9. Pluck the thick line. Listen to the pitch of the sound.

10. Hang the pail on the hook at the end of the thin fishing line. Then pluck that line. How does its pitch compare to the pitch of the thicker line?

Figure 6

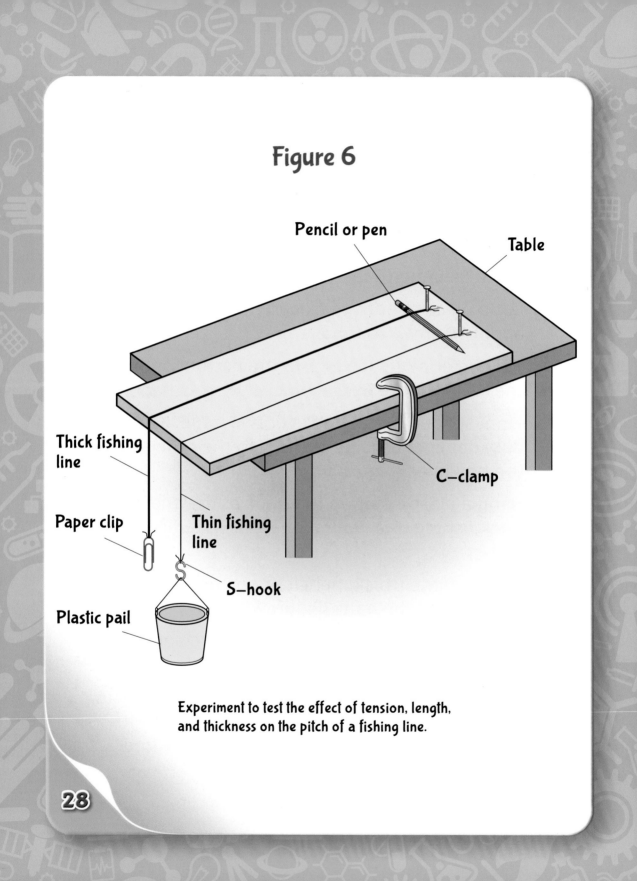

Experiment to test the effect of tension, length, and thickness on the pitch of a fishing line.

Thickness and the Frequency of a Vibrating String: An Explanation

Both fishing lines had the same length, and the tension (pull) on the line was the same when you added the pail but you probably found that the thinner line had a higher pitch than the thicker one.

Something heavy does not vibrate as fast as something lighter. You saw that in Experiment 1. The short length of ruler had less mass than the longer length and it vibrated faster creating a higher pitch. The thinner fishing line had less mass than the thicker line and therefore vibrated faster with a higher pitch.

Notice the strings on the violin. See how their thickness differs. Which strings do you think are used to play notes of a higher pitch?

How Does Length Affect the Frequency of a Vibrating String?

If you watch a guitar player or violinist closely, you will see that they constantly move their fingers over the strings on the instrument. How does this movement affect the pitch of the strings? You can do an experiment to find out.

Experiment 6: Pitch and the Length of a Vibrating String

Things You Will Need:

- board used in Experiment 5
- thick and thin fishing lines (often referred to as the "test" of the line; 6-lb test is thinner than 12-lb test)
- S-shaped metal hooks or two large, heavy-duty paper clips
- plastic pail
- water
- quart jar or measuring cup

1. Use the S-shaped hook or large paper clips to hang a plastic pail on the end of the thin fishing line from Experiment 5. Add a quart of water to the pail to provide tension (pull) on the line. Be sure the pencil or pen is still under the fishing line near the nails (see Figure 7).

2. Pluck the length of line that extends from the end of the board to the pencil or pen.

    What do you hear?

3. Find a point about midway between the end of the board and the pen or pencil. At that point use your finger to press the fishing line down onto the board, then pluck the line (Figure 7).

4. Compare the pitch of the longer and shorter lengths of line. Which length had the higher pitch? Which length vibrated faster?

5. Repeat the experiment using the thicker fishing line. Does the pitch of the two lengths of plucked line differ in the same way it did with the thinner line?

6. Try plucking even shorter lengths of both lines. Can you predict how changing the length will affect the pitch?

Figure 7

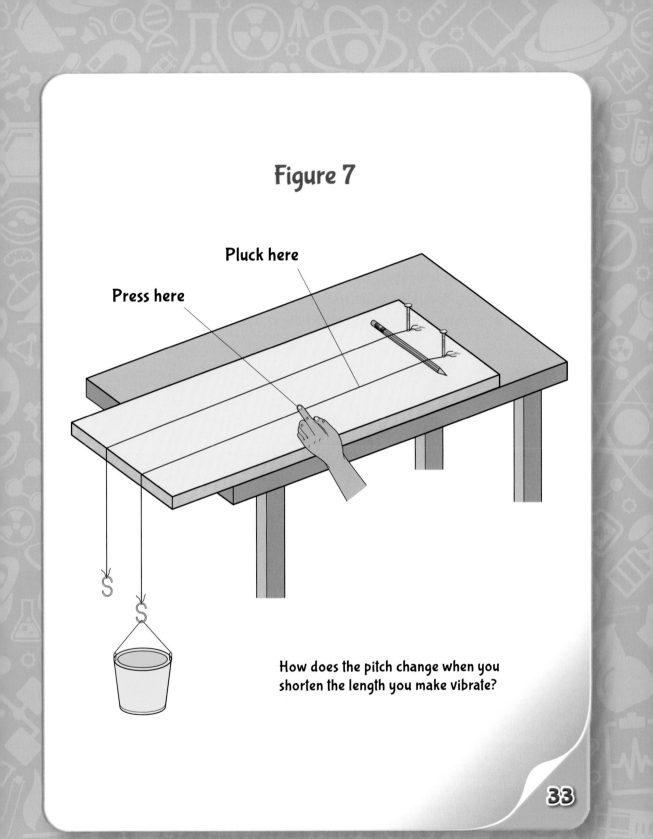

Pluck here

Press here

How does the pitch change when you shorten the length you make vibrate?

The Effect of Length on the Frequency of a Vibrating String: An Explanation

Making the line shorter increased its pitch because it vibrated faster. The effect was the same for both lines. When the lengths of the two lines were equal, the thinner string had the higher pitch because it vibrated faster. A guitarist or violinist can press on the strings of his or her instrument to play shorter or longer lengths of string and change the pitch accordingly.

How Does Tension Affect the Pitch of a Vibrating String?

In the previous experiment you saw how a musician changes the pitch of the strings by shortening or lengthening the amount of string that is vibrating. How else can he affect the pitch of his instrument? The next experiment demonstrates the effects of tension on pitch. What do you think will happen to the string's pitch when you increase tension? When you reduce tension? Let's find out!

Experiment 7: Pitch and the Tension (Pull) on a Vibrating String

Things You Will Need:

- board used in Experiment 5
- thick and thin fishing lines (often referred to as the "test" of the line; 6-lb test is thinner than 12-lb test)
- S-shaped metal hooks or two large, heavy-duty paper clips
- plastic pail
- water
- quart jar or measuring cup

1. Hang a plastic pail on the end of the thin fishing line using the S-shaped hook or large paper clips. Add a pint of water to the pail to provide tension (pull) on the line. Be sure the pencil or pen is under the line near the nails.

2. Pluck the line. What do you hear?

3. Add another pint of water to the pail.

4. Pluck the line again. Has the pitch changed? If it has, did the pitch increase or decrease? What does this tell you about the frequency of the vibrations?

5. Predict what will happen to the pitch if you increase the tension. Then add a third pint of water.

6. Pluck the line. Was your prediction correct?

7. Repeat the experiment using the thicker line. Are the results similar?

The Effect of Tension on the Pitch of a Vibrating String: An Explanation

The experiment demonstrated how tension affects a string's pitch. To increase the tension, you added water to the pail. The increased tension made both strings vibrate faster and therefore the pitch was higher.

Violinists and guitarists tune their instruments in the same way. They turn the tuning pegs at the end of their instruments. This changes the tension on the string, which changes the string's pitch or frequency of vibration.

Matching Sounds

We know that things that vibrate make sounds. These things have a natural frequency at which they vibrate. For example, on a piano, the middle-C string vibrates at 261.1 Hz. That is its natural frequency. Suppose someone plays or sings a note with a frequency of 261.1 Hz. What do you think will happen to the piano's middle-C string? You can find out by doing Experiment 8.

Experiment 8: Matching Vibrations (Resonance)

Things You Will Need:

- 2 empty 1-liter plastic soda bottles
- 1 empty 2-liter plastic soda bottle
- a friend

Wind instruments, such as oboes, produce sounds by making air vibrate. The musician is able to make the air vibrate at the frequencies of musical notes. You can similarly make sounds by blowing into a bottle and seeing what happens to the air in a nearby identical bottle.

1. Find two empty 1-liter plastic soda bottles.

2. Hold your lower lip against the edge of the mouth of one of the bottles. Blow into the bottle. With a little practice, you should be able to make a low-pitched sound. That sound is the natural frequency of the air in the bottle.

3. Teach a friend how to make the sound in an identical bottle.

4. Hold a 1-liter bottle next to your ear. Have your friend stand near you and blow into the other 1-liter bottle. (See Figure 8.) What do you hear coming from the bottle by your ear?

5. Have your friend hold her bottle next to her ear.

6. What does your friend hear when you blow into your bottle?

7. Do the experiment once more. This time have your friend blow into a 2-liter plastic soda bottle. Listen with your 1-liter bottle. What do you hear this time? What can you conclude?

Figure 8

Matching sounds have the same natural frequencies.

Matching Sounds: An Explanation

Suppose someone plays or sings a note that matches the natural frequency of a piano string. The string will vibrate with a matching frequency. It's almost as if a ghost is playing the piano. No keys are touched, yet the piano makes a sound.

You did the same thing when you made a sound by blowing into an empty soda bottle. The nearby identical bottle responded by making the same sound. The air in the second bottle responded to the sound made by the first bottle. Its natural frequency matched that of the sound, making its air vibrate. This response of a string or air column to a matching natural frequency is called resonance or a sympathetic vibration.

Making Music With Tongue Depressors

We've learned a lot about how sound works. Let's use that knowledge to build your own vibrator-type piano.

Experiment 9: A Tongue Depressor Piano

Things You Will Need:

- table or counter
- wood board
- 2 C-clamps
- 8 tongue depressors

1. Press a tongue depressor firmly against a table or counter with your hand. Let some of the depressor extend beyond the table's edge. Pluck the depressor with your other hand. The wood will vibrate making a sound.

2. Change the length that is free to vibrate. Pluck the depressor again. What do you notice about the pitch?

3. Find a board and two C-clamps. Use them to press eight tongue depressors against a table or counter (Figure 9).

Figure 9

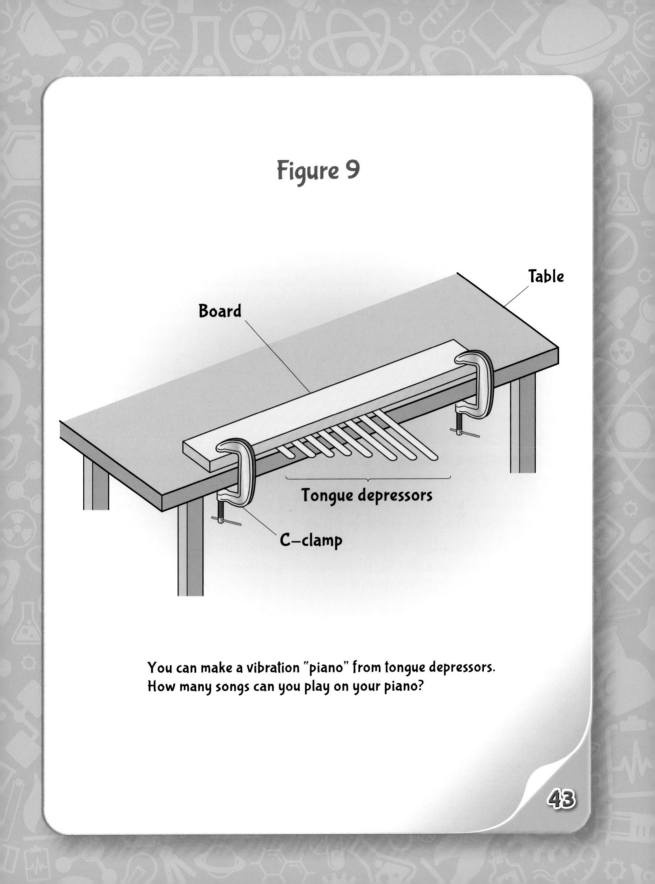

You can make a vibration "piano" from tongue depressors.
How many songs can you play on your piano?

4. Patiently adjust the length of the tongue depressors (Figure 9). When their free-to-move lengths are just right, you'll have a "piano." You can play a full musical scale—*do, re, me, fa, sol, la, ti, do.*

5. Once you have made your "piano," see if you can play some simple tunes. Maybe you can sing along!

Making Music With Tongue Depressors: An Explanation

In Experiment 1 you made sounds with a vibrating ruler. The shorter the length of ruler that vibrated, the higher the pitch. You used that basic principle to make a simple tongue depressor "piano." The shorter the length of the tongue depressor, the higher its pitch when it vibrates. With patience, you adjusted the length that vibrated until it played a note that you recognized. Once you can play a musical scale, you can have fun playing tunes on your "piano." Science is everywhere!

You may not be ready to compose a tongue depressor piano symphony but you hopefully understand a lot more about how sound is created! You can learn more about the world around you by taking a look at the other books in this series, which investigate color, light, animals, stars, and time. Keep exploring, scientist!

Figure 10

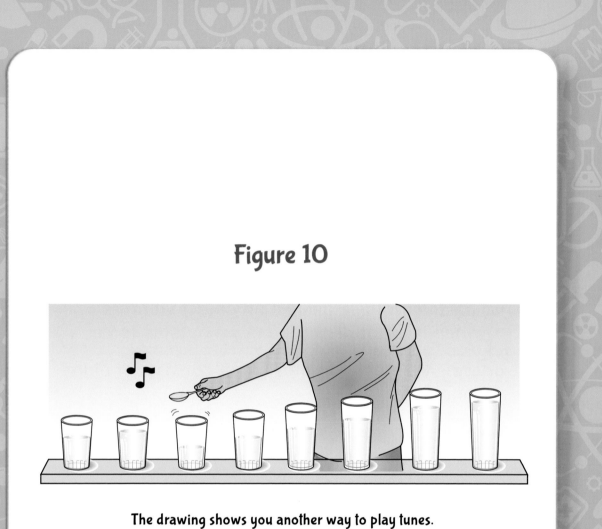

The drawing shows you another way to play tunes.
This time with glasses filled to different depths with
water. Use a spoon to play the notes.

GLOSSARY

conductor—A device or vessel used to transmit sound or heat.

frequency—The number of times something happens within a given time period.

hertz—A unit to measure frequency. One hertz (Hz) is a frequency of one event per second.

natural frequency—How fast an object vibrates when it is not disturbed by an outside force.

octave—An interval in music that consists of eight tones.

pitch—The property of sound that changes when the frequency of vibration changes.

resonance—A vibration produced by another vibration of the same frequency.

tension—Stretching something tight.

tuning fork—A two-pronged device that vibrates at a certain pitch when struck.

LEARN MORE

Books

Johnson, Robin. *How Does Sound Change?* New York: Crabtree Publishing Company, 2014.

Kessler, Colleen. *A Project Guide to Sound.* Hockessin, DE: Mitchell Lane Publishers, 2011.

Parker, Steve. *Tabletop Scientist—The Science of Sound: Projects and Experiments with Music and Sound Waves.* Mineola, NY: Dover Publications, 2013.

Websites

Ducksters

ducksters.com/science/sound101.php

Physics concepts for kids help readers understand the basic science of sound.

Science Kids

sciencekids.co.nz/sound.html

Learn more about sound with these experiments and videos.

Harris County Public Library
Houston, Texas

INDEX